Acknowledgments

Chapter One: Choices

Chapter Two: Habits

Chapter Three: Attitude

Chapter Four: Mindset

Chapter Five: Purpose

Chapter Six: Putting it all together

Epilogue

Acknowledgments

I thought writing a book was exclusive to a certain type of person. I thought I wasn't one of them. It wasn't because I didn't like reading or couldn't read. It was because I thought I wasn't smart enough. I remember reading aloud in elementary school and when I didn't read as fast as the other kids, they would make fun of me. Even later in High School and College, I would think I would do well on a reading assignment and would get a C or low B. As I have gotten older, I have become more of an avid reader and learned to realize that I could add value in this forum. I learned that my experiences may help someone else, so I wrote this book.

I wish my brother, Greg Dorsey and my father, Leonard Richard (L.R.) Webb, were alive to share this with me. They are with me in spirit and this book would not have been possible without their inspiration and belief in me throughout my life. Thanks to my sisters, Sharon Dorsey and Theresa Webb, and my mother Sadie Webb for being the family support I always needed. My love, Laura Breeding, for being so supportive throughout this journey and believing in me when I didn't believe in myself. To my children, Malakai and Shey Webb, I share this book as a testament that you can do and be whoever you want to be. I admire you both. You are the best of me.

Chapter One

Choices

"It's the small consistent things that we do every single day, those little choices we make, that literally determine if we'll experience how good our bodies are designed to feel" Devin Burke.

We can live one day at a time, and still need to be mindful about how the choices we make today will impact tomorrow. Choice. Is it really that simple? My life is as my life is because of the choices I have made. I can not excuse myself for not knowing what my choices would produce and/or blame those who withheld knowledge/access for whatever reason. However, neither will change anything about my life as it is/has been or serve to change anything about my life as it will be in the future. All any of us can do, is to make the most informed choice and learn from our mistakes, so in the future we can choose different if we want to produce different results.

As a teenager, I used to wear ridiculous clothing. I drank wine coolers and chased it with a 40oz of Old English Malt Liquor on a regular. I used to shoplift often. I also engaged in substance abuse. I was also filled with enormous physical aggression and anger as a teenager, which led me to fight rather often. I had dreams of being a big drug dealer. Someone telling me about all my potential did not affect my affinity for these death traps. I do not say any of this to glorify the unfortunate choices of my past. I say it to remind myself and you what it is all about and that is LOVE. Condemnation didn't correct me or give me an internal urgency to do right. Preaching to me about how I was living like a savage didn't inspire me to go within. But LOVE did. Until I developed self-love, I continued to make poor choices.

So, let's start with poor choices. All the poor choices I have ever made have at bare minimum served the purpose of teaching me how to make better choices. Mistakes are inevitable. Create a space for yourself and others to make them. It's ok to be transparent when you do. I have made bad choices, fallen flat on my face a thousand times or more. Those mistakes are your testimony to the world. Convey them without guilt, remorse, or distress may help someone get past their mistakes. Most of all it will free you from your past. That is the first step toward loving yourself.

We all have an impact on the world. Every day we change the world whether we know it or not. The choices we make will inspire or deflate others, they will comfort or

depress, they will uplift or burden. Never doubt that your actions and attitudes matter. You are powerful.
Every choice you make should protect your mental, emotional, and spiritual state of mind. At the same time, you will make choices that will not work out, bring you criticism, or cause conflict. The power is in the learning you take from the experience.

There are times when I gave people or events power over my choices. There were people who I wanted to be accepted by, so I made choices based on getting acceptance. There were events like people lying to me, cheating on me, or just plain mean to me that I allowed to affect my choices. There were times I put myself in position that they made choices for me. The most common form of this is when you break rules or the law. People with authority will have this power when you give it to them. Lastly, there are people who temporarily control your choices like parents and teachers. The greatest choice we make everyday is who we are going to be. Never relinquish this power. You will make responsible choices and they will be ridiculed. When I made the choice to excel academically, I was called "nerd", or I was "acting white". I never considered myself better than any person or event. I just realized that no person would be held accountable for my choices or the consequences of them. Therefore, they possess no right to the power of creating these choices. If you are to choose wisely, you must choose wisdom as a point of personal orientation. You obtain that wisdom from watching people make choices and learning from them. This may result in you picking the uncomfortable or unpopular choice. It also may result in you going without for a period, instead of choosing the immediate and path of least resistance option.

We weave our lives through our choices. Be mindful, the choices you make today create tomorrow's outcomes. The webs we weave can serve us or enslave us. Make sure you are spinning meaning in your life. Remember, everything you do is by choice and that your choices are based on what you believe is possible. However, also remember that what you believe is possible is not synonymous with what is possible, but it is also worth remembering the right choice.

Worksheet for Choices

Find a lesson in a choice you made that did not turn out the way you wanted. Life is evolving, as should our choices, reflecting on your heart and thinking about strengthening your voice what choices are you going to commit to make starting today spiritually, physically, emotionally, and psychologically?

Chapter Two:

Habits

"Are the habits you have today on par with the dreams you have for tomorrow?" Alan Stein

If you want to reach your goals or be great at anything, you must have great habits. When I was a teen, I romanticized my plans but dreaded the work and execution. This isn't uncommon. FOMO (Fear of Missing Out) is real. My parents were great. I thought they were overprotective but what I didn't realize they were that way because of their very own experiences. My father grew up during The Great Depression and was a World War II Marine Veteran. My mother grew up during the height of the Civil Rights Movement and right in the epicenter of Selma, Alabama. Combine this with an age difference of about 20 years and in an interracial relationship during the 1960's they each carried their own trauma as well as sharing some trauma. They only wanted to protect me from what they saw as a cruel world. I didn't understand this so every time I had an opportunity for freedom, I took advantage of it. I felt like any free time I had would need to be used for fun. I didn't make the sacrifices necessary to build great habits. I didn't realize I would be an adult much longer than I would be a child. The magic I was looking for was in the process of sacrifice I was constantly avoiding. The biggest habit I needed to acquire was the habit of breaking bad habits. Youth don't develop good habits because most only look at results. You must trust your ability to get results. Which means you must buy into your habits more than you buy into the results/consequences. This has two benefits: one, when you don't perform but have good habits, you still trust you to adjust; secondly; good habits most often, but not always, garner results. The easiest way to solve this difficulty: surrender the result and focus on the process. Results are never guaranteed but we can guarantee processes. The youth mind says: but why would I go through all the process work if I'm not guaranteed a result? The C.H.A.M.P. mind says: you can get lucky with results once, maybe twice, and convince some people sometimes. But if you don't have a process, you will never have consistent results. Habits are the highest form of risk management. This is the reason that approximately 80% of people who make Year end "resolutions" have dropped them by the second week of February. Unless you develop new, effective habits, your chances for that result you seek becomes smaller. You can't flip greatness on and off like a light switch.

Even in the face of inevitable defeat, you must operate as if the outcome is uncertain. Habits don't watch the scoreboard. There are habits that will drain your energy that you must eliminate. Number one is overthinking. It's important to give your brain the space to process through your thinking rather than being overcome by the emotional feeling of the brain. However, staying in the process of thinking through can cause paralysis by analysis and you never start action. Number two is living in the past. Our mistakes, our procrastinations, our celebrations by morning are gone. They are part of the fabric of our experiences, but no longer determinative. To hold onto a celebration or defeat too long is simply burning up time we could use by simply adjusting our mindset toward the place we're going, the next moment. Being in the presence of negative people is another habit we must eliminate. Negative people appear to be those who enjoy offending, regardless of the victim; those who cannot articulate well but crave a voice; and those using fear to gain control through fear. A negative person brings you down with them. Replace those people with people that will inspire you to do better. Replace them with people that will challenge you in a positive way. Replace the negative people in your life to remove those speed bumps and knock down those brick walls so you can be well on your way to success. Negative people will try to dim your light, so they are not alone in the darkness. Block them out and let your light shine.

What are the habits you need to grow? First, practice self-awareness. Know yourself, your limits, your strengths, your weaknesses, and most of all your value. You are valuable. Second, use positive self-talk. Be your own advocate. You are awesome, just make sure you really know it. Third, constantly strive to learn. Learn something every day. Learn to love learning. Number four is to seek to understand people. We may be different, but we are the same too. Before you seek to be understood, seek to understand. Doors will open when you seek to understand others. Live in the present is number five. Enjoy each day. Find the joys in each moment, it will make your journey sweeter. Number six is don't worry about the future. I'm not saying don't plan. Plan but have a plan so you don't worry. Worrying does nothing, it is the appendix of emotions. Lastly, don't regret your past. Own it. Learn from it. Use it and let it go. Don't run yourself down. You are awesome so believe in yourself. You got this. Enough said.

Worksheet for Habits

What new habits do you need to create to be the best version of you? What habits do you need to stop?

Chapter Three

Attitude

"The most important thing is this: To be able at any moment, to sacrifice what you are, for what you will become!" Eric Thomas

Our attitude is an expression of our philosophy. When you are a teen, it is sometimes a struggle because we are trying to figure out what our life philosophy is going to become. I realized early that what I do every day is more important than what I do occasionally. There is not much to control in the teenage world but so much to look forward to in the future. Every day you can control two things. Effort and Attitude. They are bound together. Never doubt that your attitudes matter. Having a positive attitude is one of the most important qualities we can have. Especially during times of adversity. Adversity changes attitudes from positive to negative because we are allowing fear to set in. Attitude determines our disposition, our concentration, and our stamina. Despite struggles, despite obstacles, despite troubles, be determined to hold a positive attitude. Honestly, before I hit my teens, I was talentless. I have been a corny introvert since the age of 5 and my nose has been the same size since that time. I have realized it was my attitude that changed every situation I found myself in and came out successful. I changed the way I looked at things. Challenges became opportunities. Mistakes became lessons. Setbacks became Do overs. I was building character. I started to utilize untapped confidence to improve my overall self-esteem. This resulted in a heightened mental attitude geared for success. I was cut from every middle school sport team that I tried out for. All of them. I used the coach's criticism as fuel. I used the teasing by students as fuel. I was going to get the most miles out of it. I didn't feel sorry for myself. I kept coming out. Most of all I kept working. The summer prior to high school I was intentional with my actions but armed myself with a positive attitude. It wouldn't matter if I got cut. I removed the outcome and just competed. I made all my sports team in high school and carved out a nice reputation as an athlete.

Not everything will go as planned. What matters most is your attitude. What will you learn from it? How will you move forward? What will you do next? Focus on the positive. If something is not off to a good start, start thinking about how you will turn it around. Will every situation turn out like my sports experience? No. I have worked hard and been denied promotions and even just simple recognition. I have watched people I knew were underserving of things get them. It is hard maintaining a positive attitude. When that happens, and it will, coupling that with a bad attitude only makes things worse. What can you do? You can create reality or describe reality. Our mental attitude begins with the habitual words and phrases we use. If we see challenges and opportunities in our life, then life is full of optimism and wellbeing. If we see nothing but problems and trouble, then we feel weak and tired. We think we are describing our experiences, but we create them. Attitude is a decision. Decide your attitude every day. Make sure it is positive, create the energy you want, and focus on the right thing.

The funny thing about life is, you can do anything you want. I'm not speaking simply of careers and outings. I'm speaking of the foundation of the fundamentals of attitude. How you see the world is how you shall feel the world. How you view what you do, effects how you do what you do. It's important how you program yourself. What we think, we shall manifest. This doesn't mean if you think of a new car, you will open the door and there will be a new car for you. This is about attitude. In today's world we must become disciplined in mind. It is a very important personal mastery. You only cheat yourself with a bad attitude. Attitude can't be faked or pretended. Your thoughts must be consistently striving to be the best version of you. Negative thinking must be trained out of your system. It will not happen overnight. It will need focused discipline. Our attitude must support our beliefs and dreams. Attitude is magnetic. When a person thinks of something, they begin to attract what they are thinking about. Say goodbye to the pull of negative attitudes. Do not allow yourself to be swept away by negativity. Work hard to cleanse your mind of negativity. Positive attitudes bring clarity and power. This power of attitude will manifest more than career moves, jobs, or even material stuff. Positive attitudes will solve challenges and protect you. It will protect and cover your family and friends. Start today. Be patient and diligent. Don't stop. You will feel it and know it.

Worksheet for Attitude

What triggers you to fall into negative attitudes? Is there a situation or relationship that sets it off? Develop a plan to replace negative attitudes with positive attitudes.

Chapter Four

Mindset

"The more concerned we become over things we can't control, the less we will do with the things we can control." John Wooden

Teenage years can be filled with fun, excitement, and adventure. They also can be filled with insecurity, rejection, and doubt. When insecurity and doubt creep in, what will you do? I have been a loner most of my life, in part due to various forms of rejection I experienced as a teen and in part due to the extreme comfort I found in being alone. The irony is the rejection is how I found my comfort in being alone. However, in order to become the best version of myself I had to leave the comfort of being alone and embrace rejection. It was the only way I could move forward. Ask yourself why you are afraid to move forward? Is it because you think you don't deserve it, don't have what it takes to do it, or are afraid of ridicule and judgment? The first and second are false, Totally. You do deserve to be successful and prosperous; you are worthy, and you are capable. Everything you need to succeed, you already have.   The fear of rejection and doubt is a mindset, most likely because of insecurities. Whatever your reasons, it is time to eliminate them.

How do you eliminate them? You start by changing your self-talk. Negative self-talk can lead to depression, anxiety, lack of happiness, poor relationships, low ambition, and so many other things. Do not beat yourself up because our brains are wired for survival. We are naturally wired to be more negative and cautious.

However, with practice you can rewire your brain to be more positive. Change your perception and your world changes. It is as if you put on a different set of goggles that shows the world in a much better way. Your perception of your environment has so much to do with you being able to interact within it in an effective and positive way, so the work is worth it. This is one of the biggest things you must master in order to set your identity and why mindset is so vital to success. You do not have to listen to naysayers, the ones who use words to trample on your dreams, or the non-ambitious ones who want you to be just like them. Allowing them to negatively impact you is your choice. Your voice should be drowning out anything negative they have to say. Tell yourself as often as you must that you can do anything you desire to do, be whomever you decide to be, and create anything you desire to create. Nothing will slow your progress and derail your dreams like a negative mindset. It's time to move forward. Stop treating past situations like baggage and start treating memories/ scars like souvenirs. Most experiences aren't negative or positive. It's our mindset as it relates to those experiences that make us view them in a specific way. Change your mindset. Grow from your experiences. It is time to recognize the merit of the struggle, to acknowledge that you will always have challenges and places of darkness, but they do not have to define us. Make a vow to change the voices in your head. Be determined to change your mindset from negative to positive, from fixed to growth, and from poverty to wealth. Choose to revolt against all odds, resistance and personal struggles; to strip the bad memories of their power; to remove negative people from your circle and replace them with those that give you positive and effective energy. What has happened has happened. Take control of your present and future. Give your power to you. The wrong mindset has pitfalls waiting for you. When I feared failure, never spoke about my challenges, stressed for not knowing things, and had no mentor but tried to be like others I was lost. I had no credibility, weak relationships, and did not have my own sense of self. I learned the hard way but let me share how you can avoid these pitfalls. First, I had to embrace challenges. Every challenge comes with its own seed for something great to come from it. Sometimes, the struggle is a key ingredient needed to prepare you for your blessing. Very few enjoy bench pressing adversity, but if you let it get the best of you, you'll never get your blessing. I started to embrace the struggle because the struggle is what makes us better. The struggle itself is the journey.

Second, I didn't view things as failures but as my learning curve. Anyone who has experienced greatness has had to endure a learning curve. Failure defeats losers, but inspires winners and winners ride the learning curve. Your mindset is where your inner freedom lies. Successful people maintain a positive mindset no matter what is going on around them. They build on their successes rather than focus on their past failures, and on the next action steps they need to take to get them closer to their goals.

Mindsets built on transparency are the strongest. Mental strength doesn't mean you avoid mistakes or even sharing them. Mental strength means when you make a mistake, you get back up and learn from it. The best way to learn is to teach. By sharing your mistake with others, you are teaching them how to avoid them. It's never over when you fall down, its over when you stay down. Our mistakes are part of the fabric of our experiences, but no longer determine our destiny. To hold onto a mistake is simply burning up time we could better use by simply adjusting our mindset toward the place we're going anyway. Move forward from mistakes with a mindset of positivity. Discovering what you were born to do requires trial and error. Without mistakes, there is neither learning or innovation. Life is about being your best, not being better than anyone else. Everyone makes mistakes. No one is spared. It's the mindset of the person that makes the difference. Give yourself a break. Self-forgiveness is so important to your mental health and wellbeing. Your mindset will allow you to self-assess. It will show maturity in answering for your own choices, behaviors, and outcomes. It will prevent you from wrongfully assigning blame. You will not only build trust and relationships; you will develop yourself and evolve as person.

Worksheet for Mindset

Think of the mistakes you made. How can you use those mistakes to do better and what learning experience can you share?

Chapter 5

Purpose

"The purpose of life is a life of purpose."

Robert Byrne

We are 100% responsible for our own sense of purpose. It can be built, strengthened, and made more inspiring every day. The bible says, "Never treat your true purpose in life as if it's one of your many options" (Proverbs 16:9). What is stopping you from stepping into your purpose? When you step in your purpose the whole universe starts to open new doors of opportunities for you. Purpose is not something you put down when you're tired. You have your own unique purpose. Nobody gets mad if roses don't provide shade, nobody wonders why trees aren't more fragrant. Circumstances will change, people in your life will come and go, but the purpose for your life will remain the same. No matter what you are going through, who stays or who leaves, you must push through to fulfill your purpose. To find your purpose, you must understand your highest values and realize your purpose is not for you, its for the world. That's right. People often confuse what we are passionate about with our purpose. Passion refers to us what drives us. Usually it drives us toward immediate gratification. However, it is not aligned with our highest values. Passion often drives us to seek a kind of perpetual bliss that is unobtainable even as we strive to avoid unhappiness, challenges, discomfort, or suffering, which are ultimately unavoidable. You can find your purpose through your passion. Passion is about interest. However, there is much more to purpose than interest. You have a unique gift that is fueled by your passion and nurtured by an unwavering sense of purpose. What would you be or do if you weren't influenced by family, friends, or fears? What makes you unique? Detach yourself from the distractions. What are your unique strengths and talents? At 15, I thought I was worthless, had no purpose, and wanted to end my life. The cause? Deep seated untrue beliefs about myself, my abilities, and my worth. Through that experience, I found my purpose and I believe, the assignment for my life. All it took was for a classmate feeling the same way I was, to ask me for help.   I just told them "you are worthy, you are capable". I guess hearing myself say that out loud made me think about my own plight. I started looking myself in the mirror and saying it repeatedly until I believed it. I thank God that I went through that experience. You are not alone. You matter and your life matters. There are people waiting for you to share your talents and gifts to the world. Through that experience I started to realize that my gift is to help people through adversity. Look in the mirror and dig beneath the surface. Love and accept what you find. Transform what you can change and release what can't. To me purpose is all about figuring out what ought to be, instead of what is in the way. Live and move with purpose more than ever. Not only to serve the world but to evolve spiritually. When your purpose is bigger than your fear of failure, beautiful things happen. Do something that scares you. Do something that makes you uncomfortable. Do something much bigger than yourself. Working hard for something you don't care about is called stress. Building what you love and attracting what you need is called purpose. If you chase after your purpose, the opportunity will find you. You are capable to be that person who brings everything, whose passion and purpose challenges everyone to be a better version of him or herself, and you'll amaze even yourself with the outcome. If you seek direction, you will find a way. Ask for strength and you will be gifted with grace. Submit to your purpose and wisdom will be gained. Leave room in your heart for the impossible. Yes, the impossible. The essence of the heart is to never give up. Because it's impossible to deny the passion of a purpose filled soul. Impossible to deny someone that isn't asking for permission to be great.

Worksheet for purpose

Define your purpose. How have you let fear hold you back from your purpose? How will you stop fear from stealing your purpose?

Chapter 6

Putting it all together

"Deal with yourself as an individual worthy of respect and make everyone else deal with you the same way."

Nikki Giovanni

Ok, so it's not quite as easy as C.H.A.M.P. seems but it's simple. But, as I've reflected, these 5 steps make the difference. They are certainly not the be all to end all but used together, they have the power to create or accelerate your growth. There is an adage that says change won't come until the "pain of staying the same outweighs the pain of changing". Just like I once did, as a teen you may feel so alone in your struggles. As a teen I know it's a time that you may not feel comfortable in your own skin. I'm not even talking about the physical changes happening to you. When I was a teen, I was doing things that wasn't me and it took me years to be comfortable. In high school, I had friends selling drugs. I was blessed because older kids would tell me I needed to go to college. When I got to college, I wasn't doing the work. I put on an image that I was handling my business. I didn't tell anybody I was struggling, I was just trying to fit in. However, the problem wasn't my lack of academic success, the problem was I was pretending like I was an academic success. Once I decided to be transparent and deal with the truth, what I noticed is instead of crumbling emotionally, I was building an emotional foundation. I stopped living a lie. The best advice I got was "Keep being you. Be vulnerable." If I didn't start living in my purpose and being me, I wouldn't have been able to accomplish things I never thought I could accomplish. Trust me I would rather feel uncomfortable pushing for better than feel uncomfortable settling for less. Social media can portray a false reality. Youth can get caught up in looking busy and acting big time. Social media allows people to put on a façade. Don't let it take the place of actual working. Don't search for the perfect moment, create it. Follow these steps to create it. You don't effectively chop a tree down by hitting a tree a thousand times. You effectively chop a tree down by hitting it in the same spot a thousand times. Start off by writing down all your ideas. You don't know which one will be the game changer. You can only catch lighting in the bottle if the bottle is open. Next, self-assessment is key. Create a structure in your grind, task list to prioritize and organize your thoughts. Write it down. People forget but paper remembers. Prioritize those tasks so you can clearly see what's important. Don't forget to dream but the dream won't get you the goal, your idea will. Examine your idea and ask yourself "What's the most effective way to get there?" Don't let the perfectionist in you suffocate the idea. Done is better than perfect when perfect is never done. I realized when I started writing this book that I had more books in my head than in any library. I wrote several books and once I got to chapter 3, I would stop because it wasn't perfect. Once I got that weak voice out of the passenger seat of the car and drove away, this book came to fruition. I never looked back. I won't pick up that weak voice again. The next one is a tough one. There are goals you are talking about for the high that you get. It's verbal masturbation. You are talking about goals for the sake of talking about goals. The high you will get from executing is the real high. Another big one is to watch how you talk about yourself. Stop defeating yourself with language and demeanors. For example, instead of saying "I'm broke" say "I am in the transition of becoming wealthy". Instead of saying "I suck at ….." say "I am moving towards being better". Lastly, instead of saying "I don't have good relationships" say "I am currently building a bridge to better relationships". Which words would you use to describe yourself? Intentional, purposeful, conscious, intentional, willful, motivated, or determined. Pick your own positive terms. Action step one: "I am (insert word) about (insert goal). Action step two: Record yourself speaking this affirmation into a video and play the recording before you go to sleep every night. You are your resume. You are a living, breathing resume. I say this to say don't just focus on what you do but focus on the level of energy you put into it. The difference between potential and performance is the amount of energy you put in it. You probably don't put a whole lot of energy in chores like doing the dishes. However, you may have a lot of energy for extracurricular activities. My son has a lot of energy for sports. He goes 120% but cleaning the house he has about 70%. He has come to learn though that if he gives 70%, we will have issues with me. He now does an energy measurement. He gets pumped to have free time not for clean dishes, so he puts energy on work. I never had energy for math class, social studies, or English. I had a lot of energy for gym and lunch period. I realized and I hope you do as well, the amount of energy you give something will determine how healthy you are, how healthy your relationships are, how much money you make, etc. Understand that how you do anything is how you do everything. Measure your energy and be honest. You may not have energy in one area. What can you do to put energy into it? You don't workout and next thing you know you're obese. You think you are being busy, doing stuff but you are not getting results. It's all because the energy you are putting into it. There is an energy level necessary to take you from being average to being great.

Epilogue

Look at the direction you want to go in and then you put a plan together and make that happen. Youth C.H.A.M.P. was developed to provide the direction. My life has been quite an adventure. There have been times when I must give myself a pep talk to get me going. My inner voice is like a coach, and it never let me give up and it congratulates me when I deserve it. What does your inner voice sound like? There will be days when you won't feel like eating right, doing homework, exercising, etc. Guess what? Those feelings will never give you results. Youth C.H.A.M.P.s is learning to conquer your mind despite how you may feel. Push yourself. No one is ever going to give you what you truly want and deserve in life. When you work hard for something, no one can ever take that satisfaction away from you. Why? Because you earned it.

Let me know how you are doing: leonard@webbolutionarymotivation.com

Get information about my coaching program:

info@webbolutionarymotivation.com

Wishing you all the success in the future.

About the Author

Leonard Chello Webb, retired Law Enforcement Professional turned youth advocate after a 27-year career in the Bureau of Prisons. He has a passionate desire to see people reach their full potential. As a popular Academic Success Speaker, his topics include youth substance abuse prevention, embracing adversity, and goal setting. He trained government employees for over 20 years in areas of personal protection, managing diversity, and dealing with difficult people. He has counseled thousands of returning citizens in the criminal justice system to help them lead healthy and productive lives after incarceration. He uses his experience now to help youth reach their potential while navigating potential/ real adversity. He continues to teach criminal justice as an Adjunct Instructor at Potomac State College

www.ingramcontent.com/pod-product-compliance
Lightning Source LLC
Chambersburg PA
CBHW071416290426
44108CB00014B/1852